POPS Mr. Twinkie:

Memoirs of My Mentor

POPS Mr. Twinkie:

Memoirs of My Mentor

JOHN MCCONACHIE

StoryTerrace

Text Michelle Booth, on behalf of StoryTerrace

First print September 2024

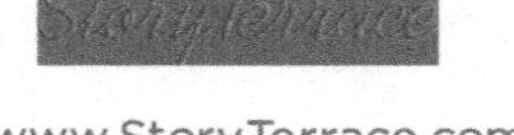

www.StoryTerrace.com

To my family and friends who encouraged me to tell my story about my grandfather's impact on my life and who have listened to my stories about him for many years.
He was an inspiring man who focused his life on his family!
My hope is that after reading about POPS, we all renew our priorities on our FAMILIES.

CONTENTS

1. MR. TWINKIE

The Twinkie. The mere mention of this iconic treat has the extraordinary power to evoke a delightful wave of nostalgia in the hearts and minds of those who hear it. In an instant, people are transported back to the innocent days of their childhood. A simpler time when devouring the golden sponge cake filled with vanilla cream was a cherished pleasure.

Maybe it was the experience of biting into Twinkies for the first time and savoring every bite. Perhaps it was the tradition of finding a shiny cellophane package of two Twinkies nestled inside a school lunch box or receiving them as a surprise treat from a doting parent or grandparent that created those fond childhood memories. Whatever the specific experience may have been, the Twinkie has a remarkable ability to reconnect people with happy, carefree moments from their youth.

While people's memories of the Twinkie are plenty, few may know much about the man behind the quintessential snack cake. He was affectionately known to the world as Mr. Twinkie. But to my family, he was Pops, a man whose presence and love shaped my life in many important ways. James Alexander Dewar, inventor of the Twinkie, was my grandfather.

Pops was born in Pugwash, Nova Scotia, Canada in 1897. He came from humble beginnings and lacked a formal education, but that didn't dampen his entrepreneurial spirit.

He immigrated to the United States at a young age and made his home in Chicago. By 1920 he landed a job as a deliveryman at Continental Bakeries. The company sold bread under the Wonder brand and cake under the Hostess brand.

Every morning, he loaded up his horse-drawn cart with bakery goods and delivered them to every grocery store and shop that sold food in the town. He took great pride in his work, and it became clear early on that he was a natural-born salesman. He was always studying his customers as he made his deliveries, so he could learn more about how they consumed Hostess products.

By the time of the stock market crash in 1929, it wasn't an easy life for anyone. People were out of work and struggling to make ends meet. Food was scarce. Many families started keeping small gardens at home and others participated in local community gardens to grow their own food.

During the Great Depression, customers were buying small, white, spongey angel food cakes from Pops. He learned that people would use the cakes to make homemade strawberry shortcake with fresh strawberries from their own gardens. This happened for about nine weeks out of the year, during strawberry season.

Continental Bakeries used special pans to produce the solid, oblong-shaped cakes, but there was no filling in them. Pops had a mind for business and realized the company's capital investment in the pans could be put to better use. He went to his company and said, "We make angel food cakes for nine weeks a year. Then, the pans sit idle until the next strawberry season." He urged Continental Bakeries to make a new product of its own. The company liked the idea, so Pops got to work. Hence, the Twinkie was born.

The original Twinkie made its debut on April 6, 1930. (April 6 is now known as National Twinkie Day.) Pops came up with the name for the new treat while on a business trip after driving by a St. Louis shoe store named "Twinkie Toe Shoes." The name Twinkie caught his eye, and hence, he named the new product after the shoe store.

Most people probably thought the first filling in the Twinkie was vanilla, but it was actually banana. The conversion to vanilla didn't happen until 1942. The United States didn't import any bananas during the war days, so Pops was forced to change his recipe. Sales increased significantly when the company made the change to vanilla, so the banana filling never returned. It was only the beginning of the taste of success that the Twinkie would bring.

The Man Behind the Snack Cake - POPS

We all have probably witnessed certain people that can just light up a room and lift people's spirits. Well, that was Pops, no matter where he went. His gift was truly connecting with people from all walks of life -- from his regular customers to people working on the factory floor at Continental Bakeries.

He talked to his family, friends, and everyone he would meet. My grandfather had a way of making people feel good about themselves. They felt they knew him, they felt appreciated, and they just loved being around him.

Pops had a stature in life. To society, he was famous. He was the man who had invented many people's favorite childhood snack cake. Yet, despite his success as the mastermind behind the beloved Twinkie, he remained grounded and humble. He was a family man through and through. Pops was the center of my family's universe and a source of inspiration, love, and togetherness for me.

Pops and my grandmother, Gay Gay, were the rock-solid foundation of our family. It's often said that the spouse is the key to success, and Gay Gay was no exception. She was a statue of strength -- both physically and in her personal character. She embodied strength and resilience, providing the unwavering support behind Pops. He was the driving force, a charismatic leader. She was the quiet but formidable wife beside him every step of the way. It was Pops and Gay Gay, joined at the hip.

My grandparents showed me the true meaning of family, and the importance of standing by each other through thick and thin. Their legacy of love and togetherness served as a source of inspiration for me that continues to guide my principles for my family today.

Pops and Gay Gay had four children: Dorothy, Shirley, my mom, Jimmy Junior, and Bobby. Between their four kids they were blessed with fifteen grandkids. Family was important to Pops, and he ingrained that same value in all of his children and grandchildren. Being one of those grandchildren, I speak from personal experience when I say that spending time with him was something I cherished. I just loved being with Pops and I had my own special relationship with him. I believe a grandparent/grandchild relationship is pretty much burden-free, with rules and discipline being left to the parents, so it could exist on a different and special level.

In the 1950s, when I was growing up, The Greatest Generation was back from winning World War II, the country was thriving, and families were close. Family gatherings, vacations with aunts, uncles and cousins were commonplace. Annual family traditions were honored and celebrated. To me, life seemed simple then and I wouldn't change those times for anything in the world.

Pops was my idol and became my role model at a very young age. We had a lot of fun together and I learned a lot from him. He taught me about the value of the family, but more importantly, he taught me about the value of the relationship between a grandparent and a grandchild.

It is my hope that through my personal stories in this book, you can get to know the wonderful man behind the Twinkie. The young boy with an eighth-grade education who went on to create an iconic product that went from zero to one billion sold and continues to touch people's lives nearly one hundred years later. The grandfather to fifteen children who filled our lives with laughter and fun memories, who mentored me, inspired my career, and helped me become the man and grandfather I am today.

Grandparents are a source of wisdom, guidance, and unconditional love that grandchildren don't get from anyone else. As technology continues to advance and increasingly takes maybe too much of the place of meaningful human connection, the unique bond between grandparents and grandchildren is critical, perhaps now more than ever. I hope the story of Mr. Twinkie, a.k.a. Pops inspires families to connect on a personal level. To set aside our worries and our cell phones and reengage with each other face-to-face. And maybe even share a package of Twinkies.

The man that created the icon of treats for the world: THE HOSTESS TWINKIE

Gay Gay and Pops at my parents home in Elmhurst. He believed in always looking sharp!

2. SWEET MEMORIES OF POPS

Halloween Treat Tradition

Pops had a one-of-a-kind Halloween tradition that landed him in the newspapers every year. While most people gave out the usual assortment of candies and chocolates, Pops handed out packages of Twinkies to the trick-or-treaters who came to his door. Word spread quickly through his neighborhood in River Forest, Illinois. Needless to say, the Dewar residence became a must-visit destination for kids every Halloween.

This "Twinkie-Treat" tradition gave people a small glimpse of the generous and fun-loving head of our family, and it made him even more of an endearing figure in the community. Pops had a gift for making Halloween unforgettable for neighborhood kids. But what truly set him apart was his natural ability to make ordinary moments extraordinary for me and my family. His presence made every day feel like a special occasion. He showed me that life is full of opportunities to have fun, and he did it effortlessly. He turned family dinners into feasts of laughter. Regular occurrences could quickly become an adventure if you were with Pops.

My Wingman

Pops and I had a special relationship. He was my grandfather, but he was also my wingman. We shared a sort of telepathy, and it never failed me.

In high school, if I liked a girl, the first thing I'd do was to take her to meet Pops. He had a magnetic personality and an innate ability to put people at ease. He showed a genuine interest in their lives. He knew the role he needed to play for me when I would introduce him to a new young lady; he played it perfectly. He was extra sweet to them and would always share with them how proud he was of me. Then, there was his subtle yet much-appreciated signature move of slipping a five-dollar bill into my wallet right as the girl and I were about to leave. This was his way of saying "Go out together and spend this five dollars on your date." The end result of these encounters was always the same: The girls liked me more when we left. What can I say? I had to play to my strengths, and he was my strength.

Pops didn't just teach me about dating, but about being genuine, kind, and supportive in any relationship. Through his own actions, he demonstrated the impact of making meaningful connections with others, in business and with family and friends. He showed me that true, genuine charisma is the opposite of being the center of attention. It's about making others feel seen, valued, and appreciated.

Family Traditions

Pops was more than just the patriarch of our family. He was the heart and soul of it. His dynamic presence defined us as a close-knit family. He was the guiding force, shaping all our activities and traditions, and the influence he had on my life was immeasurable. He made sure that these traditions were opportunities to truly connect, strengthen our bonds, and create lasting memories together.

We got together for every family member's birthday and my dad's aunts would always make a sponge cake, which was always served with Peterson's ice cream, a favorite of ours and many people living in Oak Park, River Forest area. We would gather around the cake topped with lit candles and sing the traditional 'Happy Birthday' song to the guest of honor. As the singing came to an end, Pops added his own unique touch. Full of enthusiasm, he would exclaim, "Speech, speech!" It was his trademark finish that never failed to bring an extra cheer to the celebration. It became a family tradition that I carry on with my own children today.

Christmas Eve was a special occasion in our family, and we always gathered at Pops' house. Spending time together and exchanging gifts were a big part of the festivities, but we also loved eating the humble German dish known as mulligan stew. It was my grandmother Gay Gay's family recipe, and she made it for us every year. The simple meal of spaghetti, a little slice of onion, celery, and some hamburger meat fed a lot of people for a relatively small amount of money. We loved Gay

Gay's stew so much that we even wrote a song about it, which also became part of our family's Christmas Eve tradition. The song went like this: "Mulligan, mulligan, mulligan stew . . . it's good for me and good for you . . . "

Vacations were another family ritual we all looked forward to. I can't think of any vacations we took that didn't include my aunts, uncles, and cousins. That's how it was in the '60s. Family was important to people, and spending holidays, birthdays. and vacations together was a high priority. Year after year, like clockwork, Pops and my uncle Kent -- my aunt Dorothy's husband -- orchestrated everything for all our vacations. We went to the same places every year. There was the High Noon Beach Resort in Lauderdale-by-the-Sea, Florida. Pops and Gay Gay always stayed in the same room each year, room one, which had an oceanfront view. We had a lot of fun at the beach, and we played a lot of shuffleboard, which always got very competitive.

Another beloved destination was Manitowish Waters, Wisconsin. In the summer we packed our suitcases and headed to Voss' Birchwood Lodge, a resort that's now over a century old. We did a lot of fishing there, especially for muskie and walleyes. Besides being an ideal location for our annual family getaways, Manitowish Waters is known for being the town where the infamous John Dillinger and his gang had their shootout with the FBI at the Little Bohemia Resort. Universal Studios filmed a movie about it called *Public Enemies,* starring Johnny Depp as John Dillinger.

Pops and my uncle Kent also made Easter an extra-special holiday that my cousins and I would eagerly look forward to every year. Kent turned a typical egg hunt into an adventure by hiding different amounts of money inside plastic eggs. If you grew up in the '50s, you know how excited a kid would be to find an egg with a quarter in it or, if they were really lucky, a dollar bill. It was a lot of money for a kid back then and we just loved it. The family competition was fierce, but it was all in good fun.

A Spirit of Competition

Our family vacations, holidays, and birthdays with Pops at the center of them all, were a testament to the values Pops instilled in all of us, the importance of tradition, and strong family bonds. Yet there was one bond in particular that shaped all our lives, and that was the undeniable spirit of competition. Whether it was one of our epic scavenger hunts at Easter, playing shuffleboard on our family vacations to Florida, or just a spirited board game, everyone was always in it to win.

Pops' two sons were accomplished athletes, so sports were a big deal in our family. One of my uncles was an All-American football player at Indiana University. He also played in the College All Star game against the pros, which took place at Soldier Field in Chicago every year. Uncle Jim eventually went on to play professional football for the Cleveland Browns. Uncle Bob was quarterback for Rochester University in New York. So, as I grew up, playing sports and being competitive were a significant part of my family's culture. We were avid fans, too. Pops took us to see the Chicago Cubs play baseball and the Bears play football. We always rooted for both teams.

Having two star athletes in the family forced us all to sharpen our game and always play to the best of our abilities, which was especially true at our family's annual football game on Thanksgiving Day. Playing against my uncles was tough, and they didn't take it easy on any of us! But their talent only motivated me to give it my all and show them I could hold my own on the field.

Those annual football games were a family tradition we all enjoyed, but they also taught us valuable lessons about resilience, sportsmanship, and the ability to push ourselves to our limits. We learned how to handle both defeat and victory with grace and determination, which I feel helped shape my personal character. Experiencing both wins and losses taught me humility. It made me appreciate the value of hard work and understand that success wasn't just handed to you. You had to earn it. Like Pops, my uncles were role models who encouraged me to strive for excellence in everything I did. Believe me, we lost a lot playing against my uncles.

Although Pops didn't participate in sports, his competitive spirit came through in the sales arena. He had an incredible work ethic, an uncanny ability to connect with people, and an unmatched drive to achieve his goals. He showed me that success was the result of hard work, commitment, and a desire to be the best at whatever you were trying to do.

His passion was contagious and made me constantly push my boundaries and strive for excellence in my career and my personal life. He set the standard for our family with his honesty, integrity, and by always treating others with respect. Pops influenced my values and behaviors that fueled my determination to be the best in whatever endeavors I pursued.

A Tractor Accident and Pops to the Rescue

My dad ran a construction company when I was in high school, I worked for his company in the summers. I was at a construction site one day, driving a tractor with a big sweeper attached to the front of it, cleaning off a street. I was your typical flaky 16-year-old who was daydreaming as I drove along with my legs dangling down. All of a sudden, both of my feet were pulled into the back tires. I couldn't break either foot loose to step on the brakes, so the only thing I could think to do as my legs were being torn up was to lunge forward and turn the key, which shut off the engine. I sat there, stuck, not knowing what to do next, when another worker, Smitty, ran over and picked up the tractor and freed my legs. My parents were off-site having coffee together at the time, so someone called them to say that they were taking me to the hospital.

My parents were already at the hospital by the time I got there. My left leg was all chewed up from the flywheel and bleeding. The doctor examined me and then left me in the room to go speak with my parents. They breathed a sigh of relief when the doctor told them I was going to be all right. Then my father came into the room, took one look at me, and said, "You're fired." Stunned, I said, "What?" He repeated, "You're fired, you're done, and so is your brother. You're both done." My mother had basically told him our construction jobs were too dangerous and that he had to fire us. Mom was the boss when it came to the kids!

I was raised to work hard, and now I was suddenly unemployed. I had no idea how I was going to find another job. This was in 1966. The country was in a recession and summer jobs were nonexistent. But once again, Pops had my back. I told him what happened, and he told me, "Come on down to the bakery."

The Hiring Process

Once my injuries had healed, I went to the personnel office at Continental Bakeries. There was a sign on the wall outside the door that said, "No summer help needed. No openings. Do not apply." Well, I walked in anyway because that's what Pops had told me to do. There was a lady sitting at the desk. She looked at me for a minute and I could tell she was wondering how I hadn't seen the sign in the hallway. She said they weren't hiring. I told her that I had seen the sign, but that my grandfather thought I might like to work here and told me to apply for a job. She looked at me skeptically and asked, "Oh really? And who might your grandfather be?" When I told her his name was James Dewar, she was happy to help me.

Without saying a word, she stood up from her desk, walked into a nearby office, and closed the solid wooden door that said "Personnel." She was in there for four or five minutes and then came back out with the man from the office following behind her. He walked toward me with a big smile on his face and stuck his hand out to me saying, "John, it's so nice to meet you and we have a great job for you. You can start whenever you want. In fact, if you have some time, I'll show you around the bakery myself."

Right then I understood the meaning of clout, and I thought it was pretty great. Pops had cleared the way for me to get an interview, but I knew I would still have to work hard and do a good job. I would never want to let my grandfather down.

Behind every great Pops is an even greater Gay Gay

The Hostess Story

After more than half a century, quality and freshness remain the most important ingredients of Hostess snack cakes. This delicious American tradition began around 1920, when people got their first taste of Hostess cupcakes with creamy filling. In 1930, Jimmy Dewar gave the public a morale boost during the Depression when he created a tasty new shortcake snack. The new creamy filled treats sold two for a nickel. When the young baker walked by a billboard advertising "Twinkle Toe Shoes," he found the perfect name for his new snack, and it quickly became America's most popular snack cake, Hostess Twinkies.

In Jimmy Dewar's days, Hostess cupcakes and his new taste sensation, Twinkies, were filled by hand – one at a time! As more and more people discovered Hostess products, production methods had to be updated to keep up with the demand. But the original commitment to quality has never changed.

By the 1950s, television sets joined Hostess cakes in millions of American homes. Hostess co-sponsored the popular "Howdy Doody Show," and Clarabell the Clown delighted the children in the studio audience by handing out Twinkies. Much later, Archie Bunker never let Edith forget to put his daily Twinkie in his lunch pail.

Three generations of Americans have enjoyed billions of Hostess snack cakes. Just about everyone grew up with Hostess cakes and has great memories that return with every bite of soft, moist cake and sweet, creamy filling. And each delicious Hostess snack is made today with the same care and concern for quality as they were when you – and your parents and grandparents – first enjoyed them as a child.

America's Favorite Snack Cakes

Twinkie multipack product cover tells everyone the story about Pops and his invention

EXCHANGE

WHY WE CAN'T STOP EATING TWINKIES

A Business Story

Ex-Wells Executive Avoids Jail Over Fake Accounts

Hollywood Writers' Strike Tests Solidarity

The Teenager of Stock Trading, Robinhood Thinks It Can Grow Up

POPS would have been so proud to see this WALL STREET JOURNAL full page article about THE TWINKIE

3. A NOBLE PROFESSION

Pops showed me the value of hard work, discipline, and the pursuit of excellence in my personal and professional life. His work ethic was second to none and he approached everything he did with a sense of purpose and dedication that inspired those around him. Whether it was talking with people on the bakery floor, taking care of customers, or increasing sales, he demonstrated everyday that true success has to be earned through effort and commitment.

A big part of Pops' job for Hostess was observing how his customers used his products. When Twinkies came on the market in 1930 they had no preservatives. That meant the original shelf life was less than 5 days. It didn't take Pops long to notice a problem with distribution. Store owners would place an order for a certain number of Twinkies, and once the cakes were in their possession, they belonged to the store. Pops no longer had a say in when to stop selling them.

It's important to remember the context of those times. In the 1950s, the concept of the nuclear family was at the forefront of the American way of life. Women stayed home and raised the kids and were referred to as "American Housewives."

This was when Pops's focus was the American Housewife. He wanted Twinkies to be a part of the bag lunches that moms made for their kids to take to school everyday. He knew he had to guarantee that Twinkies were always as fresh as possible when purchased from the stores.

This was when Pops came up with the idea of "freshness dating" for Hostess. Under this new system, he would deliver orders to the store owners, then return there in five days with a fresh batch of Twinkies to replace any that hadn't sold. The store then had a consistent supply of fresh product, and Pops ensured that shoppers received only the best and freshest quality. His commitment to providing only the best for what he considered to be his most valuable customer was the driving force behind his freshness dating. It was the key to his success. He invented the product and then insisted that it never be sold stale.

He would rather take unsold Twinkies back and replace them with fresh ones. My grandfather was definitely on the forefront of product dating.

As the popularity of Twinkies soared, Pops became a relentless advocate within Hostess for freshness dating system. He often addressed his growing national sales force, emphasizing that the American housewife was the toughest customer they would ever encounter. His message was clear: stale Twinkies were unacceptable, and simply wouldn't sell. He knew that to earn and keep the trust of the American housewives, they had to deliver fresh and delicious products without fail.

His determination to ensure the freshness of Twinkies was not just good for business, it was a matter of pride. He wanted American housewives to enjoy the same great taste and quality every time their family bit into a Twinkie.

Upholding the standards was a commitment to them and another example of his dedication to excellence. Under Pops' leadership, Twinkie sales grew from 0 to over one billion sold in a single year.

By the way, those unsold Twinkies did not go to waste. In a resourceful and rather unusual move, Hostess gave them to the Chicago Stockyards, where the hogs got to enjoy them too.

My First Lesson

I remember the 50th anniversary of the Twinkie like it was yesterday. It was a momentous occasion for Pops and the press covered it in a big way. Pops' picture appeared in hundreds of newspapers across the country and TV stations all over Chicago wanted to interview him. There is one interview in particular that I remember vividly. It took place in Pops' kitchen with Frank Mathie from ABC. He interviewed him for the 10 o'clock news.

At one point, Frank asked Pops about the public perception that Twinkies aren't good for you. Frank mentioned that some people considered it junk food and that people shouldn't be eating them. Pops, without hesitating, leaned forward and responded, "Frank, thank you for asking that question. That simply is not true. Take a look at me. I'm 83 years old, and I invented the Twinkie in 1930. You should know that I've been eating two of them every day since I invented them, and I'm just fine."

I called Pops the next day to congratulate him on his TV appearance. I couldn't help but mention the comment he had made. "They asked you about Twinkies being junk food and you told them you eat two a day, but, Pops, I'm not sure you still eat two a day."

He taught me a lesson that day that I would carry with me for the rest of my life.

His message to me that day was clear. Salesmanship is about confidence, passion, and believing in your product. It's about highlighting the strengths of your product and sharing your belief in it with others, and sometimes that means painting a picture that captures people's imaginations. By the way, he enjoyed all the hostess products and lots of candy too.

I was in sales for over 45 years, 27 of those years with Baxter Healthcare and 17 with Roundtable Healthcare Management. In 1985, the year my grandfather passed away, my company, Baxter, merged with American Hospital Supply (AHS). AHS was led for many years by a man named Karl Bays. Karl believed in the value of sales to the success of the overall business and how critical sales are to a successful company. Karl insisted that if people working at AHS wanted to get ahead in pursuing corporate leadership roles, they must, as Karl would say, "carry the bag first." Since Baxter was merging with American, I realized that this newly merged company would place the proper value on sales forces. I was a happy man.

I had the privilege to work for three gentlemen at Baxter and then later for them when they started a healthcare private equity firm. The founding date for their firm was February 5th, 2001 -- Pops' birthday. Private equity firms didn't have sales executives on their corporate staffs, but the founders felt strongly that they wanted a salesperson on their leadership team. It reinforced what Pops had been teaching me all along, that sales is an important part of business and a good thing to have on your resume. I was honored that they selected me to serve in that role for them at Roundtable.

Learning from Pops

The 50th anniversary of the Twinkie, especially that conversation with Pops, was a pivotal point for me. I was just getting started in sales and I was doing well. Pops was very interested in my career, and I continued to look to him for guidance. I would go to him often for advice. I admired him and wanted to follow in his footsteps. His support gave me much-needed confidence.

There's a common misconception that anyone can be a salesperson. It's true that people can give it a shot, but that doesn't mean they'll all be successful at it. It's not easy to exude confidence and success while staying humble, but Pops had mastered it. He was living proof of how to succeed in sales, and I wanted to learn everything I could from him. What set him apart in sales and in life was his genuine desire to help others. In a profession where making a sale often can come down to a transaction between a buyer and seller, Pops took a different approach. For him, it was an opportunity to meet the needs and standards of the American housewife in a long and endearing relationship. He often said his customer was the toughest customer on earth, so if he disappointed her, he would be in deep, deep trouble. She would stop buying if the Twinkie didn't meet her standards.

Before I even started my sales career, Pops would say, "You know, John, nobody but nobody makes more money than a good salesman." My response was, "Really? Doctors, lawyers -- no one else?" He'd say, "No. Salesmen."

The sales profession in general wasn't necessarily held in high regard. But to me, because of Pops, it was. People would associate sales with pushy tactics for questionable products. That was the exact opposite of Pops. He showed me that sales could be a noble profession based on trust and genuine care for the customer.

There was something about Pops, a charisma that just came naturally to him. People couldn't help but be drawn to him, and when they were around him, they felt good about themselves and wanted to work harder and achieve more. When he walked into the factory at Continental Bakeries, the workers all felt like they knew him. He would walk around and say hello to everyone putting the packages of Twinkies together, and he let them know how much he appreciated them.

Pops was the quintessential salesman -- no doubt about it. He always wanted to make a statement, and he did it with style. He took pride in his appearance and wore a suit and tie every day, complete with black socks and garters. It didn't matter if it was a regular workday or a family get together; he was always in a suit and tie. His dedication to his appearance was a reflection of his character. He taught me that excellence wasn't limited to your career, but that it extended to every area of your life.

I learned how to interact with people on a personal level from Pops and to treat everyone with the same level of respect, whether they were customers or not. I believe these are characteristics of a true salesperson and what sets you apart from the stereotype. That's how you get to know your customer intimately, and when you have that intimacy, there is mutual trust and it's much easier to do business together. Pops saw people as more than just potential customers. They were individuals with needs and high standards, and he took the time to listen and understand them.

Pops showed me how important it was to conduct yourself with kindness around the people you interact with. People need to trust you and rely on you. If they need you, they need to know you're there for them. Humility was a mark of strength to him, and he practiced it in all areas of his life.

Despite his incredible success, Pops wasn't one to talk about himself. I never once heard him brag about anything he did. His modesty made a big impact on me. It was a reminder that true greatness is about your ability to be uplifting to others. He was my mentor and he lived out the principles he taught. He led by example and his actions spoke volumes.

Pops cherished family. Spending vacations, birthdays, and holidays together was the norm. Being together all the time meant that my moral fiber and character were constantly on display. Pops made it clear that my reputation was my most prized possession and that it was something I had to safeguard. It was a reflection of myself, but also my family values.

Growing up in a family that thrived on sports was a defining aspect of my upbringing. We had healthy competitions where there were winners and losers. I learned how to be a gracious winner, or loser. You tried to win more often than you lost.

Looking back, I can see how those early experiences playing football, shuffleboard, and board games helped me in many ways throughout my life, especially my future in sales. I learned about discipline, dedication, and perseverance. Winning was a product of hard work, teamwork, and strategy. You may get lucky every once in a while in sales, but luck was rare. It takes setting goals, preparation, and collaboration to achieve real, lasting success. Competing in sports, with respect for your opponents, also extends to the sales arena. There is no doubt that the competitive culture I grew up in was an asset for me. I could put my abilities to good use while striving for excellence, working as part of a team to achieve a common goal.

It's not enough to have a competitive edge in sales. You also need to be a person of personal strength of character and someone your clients can rely on. Trust is the foundation of any successful sales relationship. I wanted my product to be the best choice, but I also wanted clients to view me as their trusted advisor. My career was based on one core principle: To have a reputation that would allow me to sleep soundly at night, knowing I've been honest and true in all my dealings.

Pops modeled this both in his work and as the head of our close-knit family.

I applied the lessons I learned from him and went on to have a successful career in sales for more than four decades. I knew that being a good salesman went far beyond closing deals and meeting targets. It was just as important to build relationships, make people feel valued, and encourage them to do their best. I wanted to be the kind of salesperson that had a positive impact on people, just as Pops had done. I couldn't have had a better mentor in my career and in life.

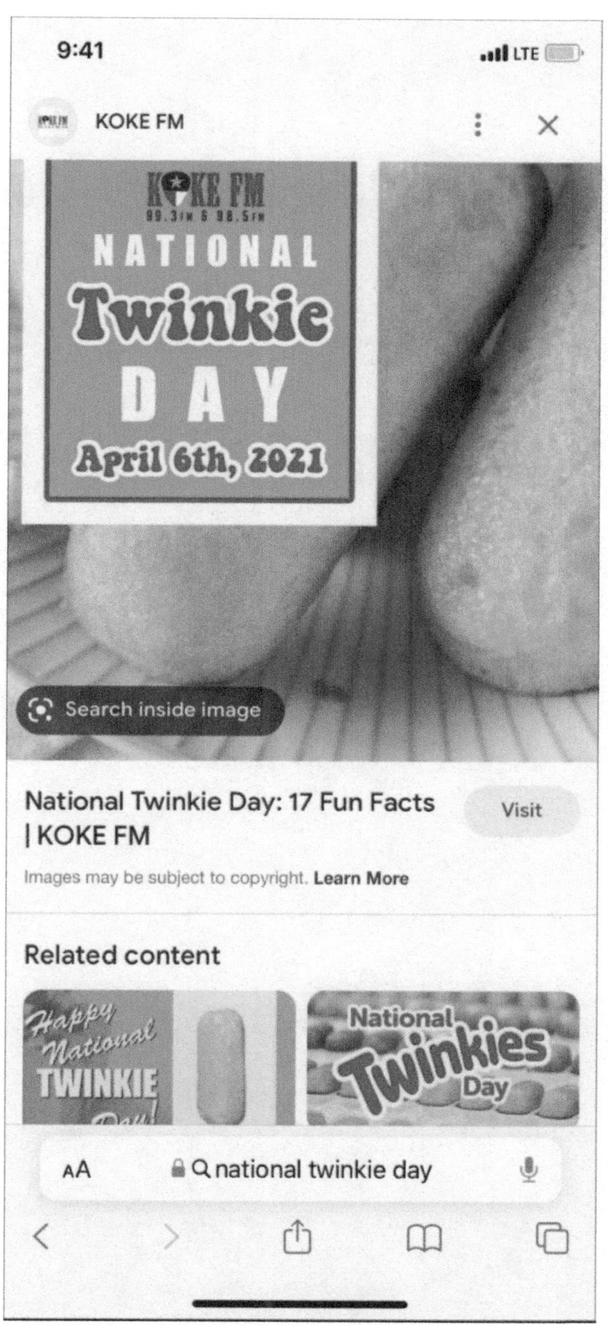

National Twinkie Day. The Twinkie turns 100 on April 6, 2030.

4. A NEW ERA

It's important to mention that Pops had an unwavering commitment to the classic two-pack format of the Twinkies. He would have never allowed a departure from this classic combination. Never. He was against the idea of selling them in any other way, or any other flavor, despite the potential for increased sales. Think of all the varieties of Twinkies that are available today. Pops would never have gone for that. He was selling a product with no preservatives, so it wouldn't have worked. He understood that the American housewife would stop buying Twinkies if they were stale and didn't meet her expectations. Anything other than the classic product would put his freshness dating concept at risk in those days.

Pops worked for various owners of the Hostess brand for more than 50 years. Over the years he advanced to the position of executive vice president of sales for the entire company. It was evident that he had a lot to contribute, and he was valued for it. By the time he reached the age where most of his contemporaries were easing into retirement, Hostess brand simply wouldn't let him. If Pops started to mention retirement, Hostess staff members always talked him into staying, and I can't blame them. He was so essential to the company's success, and the leader of sales for his entire career. He finally retired at 75 years old.

Sweetest Comeback in the History of Ever

Hostess had gone through several acquisitions over the years, struggling to survive along the way. International Telephone and Telegraph Corp. (ITT) bought Hostess in 1968, then Ralston Purina in 1975. Two decades later, Ralston sold Hostess to Interstate Bakeries Corp., making Interstate the largest independent baker in the United States. After filing bankruptcy in 2004 and then again in 2012, Interstate finally shut down its factories, much to the disappointment of Hostess fans everywhere. They couldn't believe they could no longer find their much-loved childhood favorites in grocery stores, convenience stores, or anywhere else.

Thanks to two private-equity firms, Twinkies were only out of production for about eight months. In 2013, billionaire Dean Metropoulos, one of the investors, saw an opportunity to bring the Hostess brand out of bankruptcy with a new supply chain strategy. I'm convinced that the allure of the Twinkie played a significant role in his decision to acquire the Hostess brand.

There was a lot of turmoil as he started to turn the business around, but there was also a lot of excitement. I couldn't help but think of Pops during all of this. He was a big part of the Hostess legacy, and I knew he would be proud to see Twinkies make a comeback. It meant a lot to me and to our entire family.

Hostess held a press conference at the bakery where I worked as a teenager in Schiller Park, Illinois, to announce the comeback of the Twinkie. I had the privilege of joining Dean as one of the speakers that day. It was an incredible opportunity, and I was honored to be a part of it.

It was a sizable business transaction, for sure. But to our family, it was the dawn of a new era and an opportunity to connect with the people that had dedicated their lives to Hostess. I spoke for a few minutes about my memories of working at this bakery and how happy Pops would have been at the return of the Twinkie and the other Hostess brands. I let the factory workers know how much it would have meant to Pops knowing that they were all going back to work. I ended by expressing my gratitude to Dean for everything he did to make all of that happen. Thanks to him, a beloved part of American culture wasn't going away; it was coming back stronger than ever. It was a moment my family and I will never forget.

Dean recognized an opportunity to engineer a complete overhaul of the supply chain, which had become complicated, inconvenient, and bad for business. He closed down most of the plants and implemented a new, less expensive distribution strategy around centralized baking, and warehousing. It was a game-changing move.

Gone were the days of the little Hostess trucks going from store to store to distribute products. Twinkies, cupcakes, Suzy Qs, Ho Hos, and Ding Dongs were now being carried by the biggest trucks available. Distribution began in the late 1920s with Pops, the salesman, stopping at every corner store with a cart and a horse. Now the process involved semi-trucks and centralized distribution.

Within two years, Dean's vision and determination transformed the company from a $400 million venture into a business valued at more than $2 billion. It was nothing short of remarkable.

At the time of this writing, it was announced that The J.M. Smucker Company, best known for making jams and jellies, acquired Hostess Brands for $5.6 billion. The deal closed on November 7th, 2023.

I had the privilege to speak at the 2013 press conference on behalf of my grandfather.

POPS would have been so proud to see the TWINKIE return. It was THE SWEETEST DAY IN THE HISTORY OF EVER!

Katie, my niece, who attended the press conference on July 15th 2013, the relaunch of the Twinkie!!

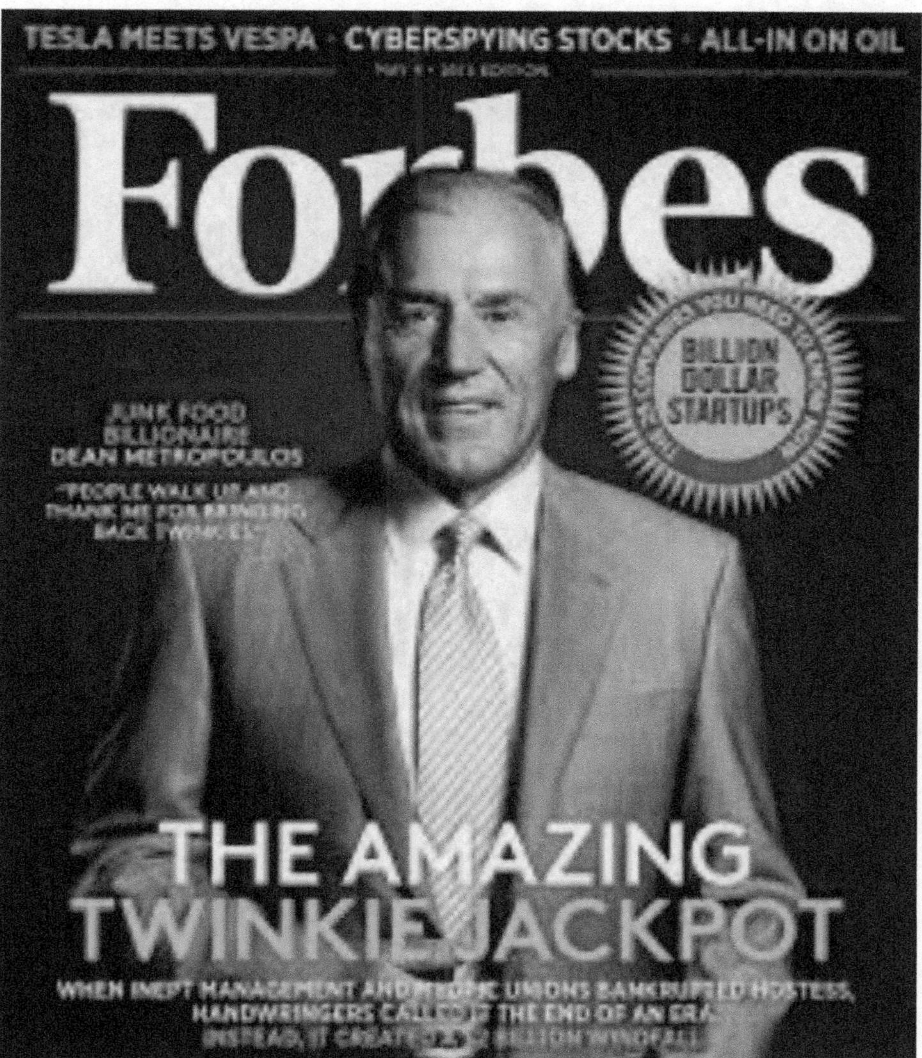

Forbes magazine cover of Dean Metropoulos who led the investment to bring Twinkies back to us!!

Here they are!!! The first production in 2013 marked the BEST COMEBACK IN THE HISTORY OF EVER!!

5. TWINKIE MEMORIES

Twinkie Dumper Job

I may have gotten my summer job at Continental Bakeries because of Pops, but that didn't mean I had any special advantages. And I didn't want any, either. I had one of the toughest jobs in the factory and I remember the long, grueling days like they were yesterday. But, come on, I was making Twinkies, after all!

Every day, without fail, I stood right at the end of the Twinkie production line, ready for action. The golden treats rolled out of the oven, still piping hot, onto a conveyor belt suspended from the factory ceiling that we appropriately named "the racetrack." The Twinkies were in 4-foot long, heavy trays made of steel and aluminum, with two rows of 18 Twinkies per tray. They traveled down a ramp, starting to cool off as they moved along, and came to a stop in front of a big vat full of vanilla cream. Then, pressure hoses would shoot the cream into each cake. It was a precise operation and happened at a fast pace.

After that, it was my turn. The cream-filled Twinkies quickly arrived at my station, and I had only a few seconds to grasp the heavy tray, and with a practiced motion, flip the tray in the air and slam it face-down onto the conveyor belt. I had to use a lot of force to make sure that none of the Twinkies stayed stuck in the tray. From there the cakes traveled down to a wrapping station where the ladies wrapped them in cellophane, and the pans went up to the wash station. It was a nonstop cycle of action.

Because of the way they timed the conveyor belt, there was a mere few inches between each tray coming to me. I did not want to be the one responsible for slowing things up, so I was flipping those trays nonstop for eight hours a day. It was tough work, but I had a lot of fun.

I continued working at Continental Bakeries for several more summers and had a few other jobs there. One was putting the squiggles on the top of the Hostess cupcakes. I also worked in the Ho Ho room. Everyone wanted to work in the Ho Ho room because it was air-conditioned and the rest of the factory was extremely hot. The work was physically demanding, especially handling the weight of those Twinkie trays, but I absolutely loved it.

We were always taught that we had to work. Our summers were not free when we were in high school and college, and there was no doubt about it. I didn't want to get fired twice, and I especially didn't want to let Pops down. So I took my job at the Twinkie factory very seriously.

People knew who I was there, but they treated me like they would anyone else, regardless of who my grandfather was. I liked it that way. My co-workers were fantastic people. We bonded on coffee breaks and lunches. "Oh, you want a Twinkie for lunch? How about one that's 10 minutes old?" We could help ourselves to whatever we wanted, so I'd grab a few cupcakes and Twinkies with my fellow bakery workers on our breaks and lunches. I enjoyed working with them and I think they enjoyed working with me too.

It was hard work and long hours, but there was also some occasional mischief. Like the time I worked on the pie line. I handled the pies after they had been filled with fruit. They'd come down the line, folded over and filled, and I'd pick them up and place them on the conveyor belt. Then they went into the fryer and would come out the other end all crispy and golden. They traveled about another hundred feet to cool off and then went to the wrapping machine. We made three flavors -- cherry, berry, and apple.

I usually worked the morning shift, but a few times I would work two shifts and get home around midnight. One night, my co-workers and I decided to have a little fun. We took some of the cherry pies and sent them through the wrapping machine that had the apple paper. It was a bit mischievous, but we did it for the fun of it, probably switching two or three hundred pies.

Anyway, years later, in Nashville, I was sharing some of my Twinkie stories with friends over dinner when one person chimed in with his own story about a fruit pie. He said, "You know, John, years ago I bought a pie with an apple wrapper, but when I opened it, for goodness sakes, the pie was cherry!" I thought he was pulling my leg, but he insisted it really happened. That's when I enthusiastically confessed, "I made that pie!" Hey, I guess it really can be a small world.

Football & Twinkie Pants

I have collected my fair share of amusing Twinkie stories throughout my life, several of them from college. My cousin Peggy and I attended Drake University in Des Moines, Iowa, and we were both part of the Greek life on campus. She was in a sorority; I was in a fraternity. During rush, our two houses had a unique tradition. Instead of serving the usual refreshments, ours were courtesy of Hostess. A Hostess truck driver would pull up and unload a giant cardboard box full of cupcakes, Suzy Qs and, of course, Twinkies. It was a huge hit with our potential pledges.

I continued to work part-time for Continental Bakeries during college. The bakery pants I wore to work were incredibly lightweight and designed for our comfort during our hot shifts. I got so accustomed to wearing them, even while playing flag football at Drake. It definitely wasn't your typical football attire. Flag football involves grabbing a flag from the body of your opponents to stop them instead of tackling them. We played in the fall and winter months, so wearing shorts in the chilly weather was out of the question. My bakery pants were the perfect alternative. I played quarterback and it was my calling card to take the field in my white bakers pants. We had a lot of fun and won the all-university championship, too!

Twinkie-Grams

Then there are the Twinkie stories from my decades-long career in sales. One of them was when I was put in charge of overseeing my company's United Way fundraiser campaign. At the time, Ralston Purina, the dog food company, owned the Hostess brand. I called to request a thousand Twinkies for our event. The person at the bakery said, "We don't give Twinkies away for charity event fundraisers." I repeated what I had said initially but added, "Oh, by the way, my grandfather invented the Twinkie and I worked at the plant for six years myself. The United Way is a charity we are supporting, and I would greatly appreciate you giving us these Twinkies at no charge." That was all it took. The bakery was happy to make the donation.

Now armed with a thousand Twinkies, I brought my fundraising idea to life. My assistant, a few other volunteers, and I tied helium-filled balloons to single pack Twinkie and sold them as what we called "Twinkie-grams." Each one had a slip of paper with a "To" and "From" line so employees could send each other special notes. Notes like "Thanks for working together with me" or "I enjoyed working with you on the team," or whatever else they wanted to say. The Twinkie-grams went like hotcakes. We sold them for $5 each, and 100% of the money went to The United Way.

The year was 1988 and I wasn't married at the time, so I decided to have a little fun myself. I wrote a few Twinkie-grams addressed to me from anonymous employees. They were delivered to my office while I was away. When I got back, I innocently asked my assistant, "Hey, who's sending me Twinkie-grams?" She didn't know because she hadn't opened the notes. I asked her to read them and find out. She read, "John, I really admire you," "John, I love working with you," "John, I'd love to go out with you." She quickly figured out I had written the notes myself and we got a really good laugh out of it. In the end, our Twinkie-gram fundraiser was a success. We sold out and raised $5,000 for the United Way.

Shetland Islands Scotland. TWINKIES sold out! The SCOTS have great taste.

6. A LEGACY OF FAMILY

My grandfather invented the Twinkie. Of course that was awesome, and I admired him for that. But I admired him even more because of the kind of person he was and the charisma he had. He believed in the value of a strong image and personal integrity. He always put other people first, both his customers and his family. He was a man of honor, doing his job in a way that brought dignity to his profession.

As I look back, I see how different things were from the world we live in today. We didn't have the technology, the internet, social media, or cell phones that have become an integral part of everyday life today. It allowed us to focus on what truly matters, family, routine, and cherished traditions. Instead of constantly staring at screens and getting distracted by notifications, we were spending time with one another, sharing meals, stories, and experiences around the dinner table. The simple act of being together was a high priority.

Talk to most people who grew up in the '40s, '50s, or '60s, and they'll likely tell you they wouldn't wish to grow up in today's technology-driven world. Those decades were a time of simplicity, discovery, and genuine human connection. We rode bikes and played outside with our friends until the streetlights came on. We always ate dinner at the same time, and if I wasn't in my seat at dinnertime, I was in big trouble.

One of the worst things you could do as a kid was to be late for a family event, even everyday ones like dinner.

We had a lot of traditions we adhered to, and that's what my family did in those days. They were positive and fun, and we enjoyed each other's company. We had lots of picnics, always with the same food -- hamburgers, hot dogs, and potato salad, always made the same way, and Coke, not Pepsi. We spent a lot of time going to Kiddieland Amusement Park and Russell's BBQ House on North Avenue. There was Boy Scouts, Girl Scouts, and little league. There was a little structure, but it wasn't overdone. Only one team got a trophy, and it was tiny.

Telephones had cords and you couldn't tell who was calling you when the phone rang. If you didn't get to the phone in time, there was no leaving a message, so you never knew who had called you. There were four channels on TV to choose from: ABC, NBC, CBS, WGN, the local channel. The news aired at 5 pm. for half an hour and then again at 10 pm. Reading your local newspaper was probably the biggest source of information. I was our neighborhood paperboy and almost every house got a paper every day. Today, several TV channels are covering news all day long. They seem to have a special interest in politics, too. When I was young, politics was a subject I had basically no interest in. I lived in the time when family was at the forefront of my life. I felt safe and loved by my parents and grandparents. This was when my personal principles took shape and for me the time to learn how to stand up for myself and embrace the world as I grew older.

Today, I believe the convenience of technology has many positive but some potential negative effects on families. Texting and FaceTiming with grandchildren brings us closer together when we sometimes live miles apart. On the flip side of technology, people sometimes find themselves spending more time on device screens than interacting real- time and face-to-face. I believe spending time with family celebrating the joys in life like birthdays, dinners, and vacations creates opportunities to exchange stories and make lifelong memories. As we do, we gain a deeper understanding and appreciation of one another. Hopefully this will have a ripple effect and impact our communities and society as a whole.

I recently read an article in *The Wall Street Journal* that examined the shifting values in people's lives. It talked about the decline in importance of family, religion, and principles, and the rising importance of material pursuits like wealth and possessions. I didn't like what I was reading. The article stated that we are having fewer and fewer genuine human-to-human interactions. We're not going to church as often as we should. We're not having dinner together as a family as often. And we're not paying enough attention to where our kids are, who they're spending time with, and what they are being taught at school.

I believe we should take a breath and return to celebrating family relationships. Having children is a responsibility that should never be taken lightly. Children aren't just an addition to the family; they're a commitment that demands your full attention and dedication. We must do our best to bring them through their formative years to the point where they can be on their own, successful and happy. Keep things simple. Focus on the core values of family, support, and togetherness. Do your best to not let your family down.

Being a grandparent is a special opportunity in life, a chance to form bonds and create your own family legacy. If you find yourself with the privileged role of being a grandparent, I encourage you to take advantage of it. Enjoy watching as they grow and learn to navigate the world. Be there to guide and support them, and have fun creating memories together.

I learned how important this role is from Pops. In some families, grandparents can be people you visit on occasion. But in our family, Pops was a constant source of inspiration, guidance, love, and wisdom.

As a grandfather of six grandchildren of my own, I understand that my role isn't just about spoiling them with treats and toys (although that's part of it). It's about being a source of support, love, and acceptance. It's about imparting life lessons and helping to shape their character and values.

I have always been inspired by the wisdom of Jesse Stuart, an American writer and educator from Kentucky, where he taught kids in a one-room schoolhouse. In his book *The Thread That Runs So True,* he wrote that in this journey called life, it's far better to have an A in character and a C in grades than it is to have A grades and a C in character. I was a C student, so that statement really resonated with me, and I grabbed onto it. I never lost sight of the fact that what truly matters is the kind of person you are, not the letters on your academic transcript. I would choose, a hundred times over, to have an A in my personal character over As on my report card. I wrote Jesse's quote on a piece of paper and folded it up and carried it with me in my wallet for many years.

I understand not everyone shares this perspective. Many teachers and parents would not agree with this philosophy and would argue for academic excellence. I appreciate their viewpoint, but for me, the value of a strong and virtuous character far outweighs any grade you earn. This is how I raised my own children. I've instilled in them the importance of being kind, compassionate, and honest individuals above all else. It's a choice I've never regretted, and I've watched them grow into adults I am immensely proud of.

I will do the same with my grandchildren. I want to always keep very close relationships with them. These relationships are both a privilege and a gift. They are a bridge between generations, a source of wisdom and love that goes both ways. In today's fast-paced world, it's easy for connections to grow distant, especially if you're a long-distance grandparent. But I'm determined to keep the bonds with my grandchildren strong. We talk and explore new adventures and laugh together a lot.

I understand that I am contributing to the foundation of their future and the future of our family. I have loved my grandkids from the day they were born and I want to be a part of their lives for as long as I can. I aspire to be a positive influence in their lives the way Pops was for me. I want to be a guiding hand, a listening ear, and support they can always turn to. And I want to have lots of fun together.

POPS MR. TWINKIE:

POPS MR. TWINKIE:

My three granddaughters, POP'S great-great granddaughters, celebrating by eating Twinkies.

Aberdeen, Emmeline, and Palmer, "The Tres Amigas!" ready to share Twinkies with everyone!

My granddaughters seated next to the original Twinkie pans from the 60s.

Mom and Dad just after they were married on March 12th 1945. What a handsome couple.

Family Picture taken in Manitowish Waters, WI. Now my hometown !!

Opposite: Mom and Dad at Voss Resort in Manitowish Waters, WI. We vacationed there for over 20 years as a family.

Pops and Gay Gay on vacation in Fort Lauderdale by the sea Florida on vacation. Rare photo of Pops without a suit on.

7. TOUCHING LIVES FOR 100 YEARS

Pops' reputation as a beloved member of the community and across America was firmly established from the time I could even begin to understand who he was. To the world, he was the inventor of the Twinkie, the iconic treat born in the Depression era that became a household name for nearly a century.

But to me, his true legacy is something far more meaningful. He imparted a sense of strength and confidence. I had the privilege of witnessing firsthand what success truly means. He was an inspiration. He showed me what it meant to aspire to greatness, to take pride in my accomplishments, and to take ownership of my actions and decisions.

He reminded me that true success doesn't come from creating iconic products or achieving fame, but rather the satisfaction you get from making a meaningful contribution to the world. From making an impression, however small or large, that continues to benefit others long after you're gone from this life.

The enduring memories we make are the history that lives on. That is what I strive for now, thanks to the lessons I learned from Pops. His life and his actions spoke volumes. He showed us how to have a lot of fun and joy in life too. His true gift was connecting with people, and he knew that the real worth of his life was tied to the bonds he nurtured within his family.

He taught me not in words, but through the way he lived, about overcoming adversity. The solution is not avoiding it or pretend it doesn't exist. We must face it head-on, knowing that as we do, we're building resilience and character. No matter who you are, you are going to have challenges in your life. You're going to get knocked down, but you can't stay down. You have to pick yourself up and move on.

In 1980, I received my first sales management assignment and had to move to Minneapolis. Pops was living alone, as Gay Gay had passed. I began to see less of Pops. Having my own family with three kids and a more demanding work assignment led to us not seeing enough of each other. Eventually my mom and her sister decided to put Pops in a senior care center. At this point, I began to come to the realization that he was at the end phase of his life.

My last memories of him were when I would visit him at the home. He was mentally as sharp as ever and we would talk for a while. Still being Pops, he would always ask how everyone was doing and let me know how proud he was of me. The feelings I had for him and for the support he gave me my entire life will always be with me. This wonderful life with him can be best summarized in what's become a favorite song of mine by Riley Green titled *I Wish Grandpa's Never Died.* I miss him.

Twinkie Stardom

The Twinkie's enduring popularity affirms its unique status, not just as a snack, but as a symbol of nostalgia, innovation, and resilience. During its early years, the Twinkie was celebrated for its affordability, freshness, and portability. It quickly became a staple in lunchboxes across the country, as Pops dedicated his efforts to taking care of the American housewife.

Throughout the decades, the Twinkie has become part of American pop culture. It has been referenced in numerous television shows, including *Howdy Doody,* a children's program from the 1950s; the classic sitcom *All in the Family* that aired in the 1970s; and the more recent animated series *The Simpsons* and *Family Guy,* plus many others.

The Twinkie has also made its way into some of the most legendary movies in cinematic history. It had a cameo appearance in the famous 1978 movie *Grease,* perfectly capturing the spirit of the '50s era the film celebrated. The 1984 blockbuster film *Ghostbusters* took an entirely different approach, as Dr. Egon Spengler used the Twinkie as a visual representation of the "psychokinetic energy" accumulating in New York City; the scene is often referred to as the "Twinkie analogy." In the 1988 action-packed film *Die Hard,* and its sequel *Die Hard 2*, the Twinkie was a source of levity between John McClane and police officer Al Powell. These are just a few references to the beloved snack cake that continue to resonate with audiences, evoke feelings of nostalgia, and illustrate its timeless appeal.

Share Your Twinkie Story

Back in 2007, Nicolas Cage was a guest on the *Conan O'Brien Show.* When Conan asked Nicolas if there was a specific moment in his life when he realized he had a talent for acting, he began to recount a story from his childhood that involved the Twinkie. He used to ride the bus to school and was often bullied because his mother used to put a package of Twinkies in his lunch bag. The other kids wanted the Twinkies, so every day, Nicolas put up a fight, but they would always end up stealing his Twinkies away. One day, in fourth grade, he decided he'd had enough. In a moment of inspiration, he assumed a fictional character, transforming into a more confident, assertive version of himself. He climbed on the bus that day and stood up to the bullies who had been tormenting him. His bravery paid off. They never took his Twinkies after that.

Nicolas Cage's experience involving the Twinkie from his childhood is a great illustration that the Twinkie isn't just a popular snack, but a source of personal memories and anecdotes for countless people. Whether humorous, sentimental, or just relatable, these stories connect us to a simpler time and become a celebration of our shared human experiences.

As we approach the Twinkie's centennial anniversary in 2030, what better way to commemorate this milestone than by sharing these personal stories from across the country? My vision is to invite people from all walks of life, coast to coast, to share their special Twinkie stories with me, and that includes you, the reader of this book. My goal in this is simple. Give everyone a chance to reminisce about their story, and to share their experience, and strengthen our connections with one another.

Let's come together as a community and create a collection of stories that pays tribute to the enduring symbol of American pop culture. Together, we can celebrate a century of Twinkie memories and ensure that they continue to be preserved for generations to come. Pops would have loved this.

Please share your personal Twinkie story memory with me.
Email to: popstwinkie1930@gmail.com

See other stories and more information about Twinkies on our website: Twinkienation.net

I will consolidate the stories and share them with you. Welcome, Twinkie Nation!

POPS MR. TWINKIE:

50th Anniversary of POPS outside his home taken in 1980. It's on to 100 in 2030.

StoryTerrace

Made in the USA
Monee, IL
01 October 2024